GOLDEN

Inspirational Quotes and Thoughts For Life and Love

DeAnthony D. Thompson

Dedication

I would like to dedicate this book to my elders, my peers and also to the generation that will come after me. I pray that my daughter will be blessed by this book as she gets older. This book entails a mix of practice wisdom that I gained from studying, reading and also from life and wisdom from God.

Acknowledgements

I would like to acknowledge my mother Pamela McDonald and my father Anthony Thompson.

I would like to thank my buddy Sven Nickerson who encouraged me to write a book.

I would like to say a special thank you to my mentor David Bowens he also encouraged me to write this book. My mentor David Bowens said speak it into the atmosphere. It'll manifest in the future. Plant those seeds of faith with your words and be intentional about the things you say and do.

Foreword

Sometimes, great things come in small packages.

As a child, my father was my pastor. I had the privilege of hearing him preach every Sunday, and I watched him live his sermons throughout the week. When he would ask me what I learned, I could normally recall one or two simple statements that he would repeat throughout the morning message.

As an adult in the field of education, I can truly appreciate what my father was doing. I've seen students, adults, schools, and churches rally around the power of a potent statement, and the results can change lives.

Your author is on a mission to change lives too.

I've served in ministry with DeAnthony Thompson for years. His passion for God's word and helping others is contagious, and he has a sincere desire to do see others succeed.

I know you'll be blessed by these words of wisdom, so I'll wrap up this forward by asking one favor...

Pay it FORWARD.

Don't keep these literary gems to yourself. Post them on social media. Share them with family and friends. Who knows? One of the quotes in this book might be the perfect statement to keep someone going.

Thank you DeAnthony for stepping out on faith. I'm sure this will be the first of many positive books you'll contribute to the world. Keep doing what you're doing.

David Bowens
NEVER GIVE UP!

Introduction

Wisdom is practical instruction throughout History. We are fortunate to have a few examples of wisdom from Chinese Proverbs, African Proverbs, quotes from wise men and women all throughout history. Some we know, others we don't. As a young man I felt inspired by God, my creator, to create quotes of wisdom that I believe He gave me. It is my hope that these quotes will help inspire men and women for generations to come.

It's also my hope that this book leaves a lasting impact on the lives of everyone who reads it.

A special note: I decided not to do a table of content because I wanted the spirit of God to lead you to wherever you are in life and whatever you need.

Love

True love is created in the Heavenly realm and it's our duty as children of God to model that love.

You can't have true fulfilling love without true commitment.

*Love is determination mixed
with absolute will power.*

When you understand the depth of true love, created by Elohim, our creator, you can't just do away with true love because God placed love in us, as He is the ultimate lover.

Love can cross the borders of hardships.

Love can detangle the webs of lies.

Love is a burning passion of Forgiveness. It's true empathy; it's you willing to give an arm and a leg for a cause that's bigger than yourself.

Love takes a lot of time, patience, and forgiveness. You don't fall in love you grow in love.

You have to love on purpose.

Love people and you will be loved back.

Relationships
Quotes

Only thy wife should know secret things that she'll never tell and the same for the husband.

Having someone trustworthy is one of the greatest pleasures life can offer.

Couples who truly
love each other
will find a way to
figure it out.

Two people can make it, especially those with the greatest desire to meet each other's needs, as well as those who operate in constant forgiveness.

A Godly
relationship can
stretch you.

Most people treat
relationships like
life, just surfing
through, with no
plan or
destination.

A good relationship
needs a solid
foundation of
trust, commitment,
understanding, and
constant growth.

If your
relationship is
built on lust, then
it will eventually
wear off.

If you don't cultivate your relationship, then it won't grow. And eventually you will leave the door open for resentment and disdain.

FIGHT FOR YOUR
RELATIONSHIP.

Be intentional
about your
relationship!

A culture without
God and family as
its foundation,
will soon be a
culture that's
crumbling.

A Godly union involves two people who come into covenant before God Almighty, for the sanctification of His purpose.

Desire more God together and individually. Pray for your significant other because prayer is very significant to the life of every Christian.

Having a partner that can motivate you in a very respectful way is beautiful. We can't forget that Eve was Adam's help. She wasn't his doormat; she truly was his helper in all matters of life.

One thing about
relationships... no
one model fits all.
So do what works
for y'all!

Real love takes
time and effort, a
lot of effort. No
longer will words
do; NOW action has
to back it up.

A plant grows with
nourishment, a
human with
substance and a
relationship with
consistency.

Value your loved
one and value your
relationship.

Don't listen to the culture around you. It's a blessing from God to have a good person, through the ups and downs.

It is a blessing to
be in a committed
relationship where
God is the
centerpiece.

It's wise to take
your time, grow,
and to remember
that everyone has
flaws. Just be
willing to do your
part in helping the
other person as
best you can.

Never forsake
finding a good
person … that's
truly a blessing.

Relationships are
similar to fishing,
it's all about
patience.

If you really want to bond with a person, then you have to spend an adequate amount of time together. True bonding takes time and consistency.

Never go a day
without a person
you can't live
without.

There are not many
blessings in this
life that's better
than a man and his
family.

We have to build
our marriages and
our relationships
under the
inspiration of
God's word.

Every relationship
needs to be
challenged at some
point, if not for
any other reason
than to strengthen
the character of
the relationship.

Relationships over a long period of time have to be a mixture of good times, which may include some compliments, and some tough times. Truth be told, the tough times can strengthen you spiritually and build your character.

Relationships are a
delicate balance
that defines life
and keeps us
grounded.

We can't overlook
the fact that men
like to be
congratulated and
patted on the book.
If you do this,
sister with
consistency, then
you can help bring
out the best in
your man.

Relationships are always a work in progress, because as humans we're a work in progress. Everyday we're faced with something different, that's life.

If you don't see
the importance of
serving in your
relationship, then
you will limit the
potential growth of
your relationship.

Life
Quotes

The most important tool you can have in life is wisdom. It's vital for a person to have wisdom.

Wisdom is like a GPS it'll help you navigate through life, and it will even help you avoid some unnecessary pitfalls.

If you can't enjoy
the simple things
about life, then
you're not living
life.

Show me your friends
and I'll show you
your now.

I have never seen a selfish person truly prosper.

Money can change
you, having
influence can change
you, going from
average looks to
beauty can change
you. To say
otherwise is not
wise.

In America, you have
to have a strong
mind and dominating
will power. If not,
then you will
conform to the
culture around you.

Even with the tools set in place, it's hard for people to think for themselves when they've been conditioned since childhood to believe a certain type of way.

Most people just
need a shoulder to
lean on, help
without being
judged, someone to
lend an ear, to hear
their silent pain.

Sometimes you don't
know the half of
what a person may
have been through,
or in some cases,
what they're going
through but just
being there for them
can mean the world.

It's not always what you say, maybe it's your ability to listen without voicing your opinion, that's more important.

People have
emotional scars and
it takes time,
patience, and a good
friend to help heal
those silent wounds.

People admire
greatness always
remember that!

Unfortunately, that same admiration can turn into jealousy.

Coming together to serve humanity will take you further than simply striving to only serving yourself. Those who serve others live in the heart of those they have helped.

When you put chains
on a person's mind,
you control how far
they go. In fact,
you help create
their outlook on
life, slowly
determining their
destiny.

In life, we need an accountability partner, someone who will listen to us, someone who will cheer us on, and someone who can keep it real with us every step of the way.

What we deem
important can help
shape the next
generation.

You ask what's the beauty in life? I would say it's beauty all around us. Look up.

When your peace
cannot be purchased,
you really have
found peace.

We over complicate
the matters of life.
Adopt the K.I.S.S.
principle.

The greatest tragedy
in life is to a live
a life not being
aware of the
blessings from
above.

You can't rush
perfection or beauty
... takes time.

Sometimes you enjoy
the simple things
the most, that's
life.

Just being in the right place can yield you some great results. Especially when you take advantage of every God given opportunity.

If you don't have
peace, then you will
be miserable.

Take a look at
nature, and it'll
teach you a lot
about life.

Oftentimes we're so close to what it is we want; maybe it's right around the corner, even though it may not feel like it, but sometimes it is. Stay the course and keep the faith.

Don't quit.

Motivational Quotes

I have never met a champion
who didn't have championship
faith.

Stay away from people who limit your risk taking ability. In other words, stay away from people who limit your faith.

Take risks because that's what
life is about ... living in faith.

If you need the perfect
conditions, then you will never
reach your full potential.

Oftentimes, great things are
born out of adverse situations.

Stop saying, "I'll do this when I get this or that," because sometimes you have to go forth before the condition looks right.

The greats in history carved out opportunity where it seemed to be none at all. THAT'S FAITH.

We can't settle for ordinary. It's time to experience more, may the power of God be exalted in your life.

Some people have that IT factor, which may be faith or God sent. They always find a way to win and a way to be successful. Maybe they didn't come from a family of wealth or go to law school but somehow they became successful.

Don't be afraid to do something that may seem weird, or indifferent at the time. That's usually when greatness is born.

Most people are afraid of venturing into the unknown, but you can't experience the ocean if you cling to the shore.

If you do anything every day,
then it's a chance that you may
like it or do it out of habit ...
nonetheless be intentional!

Your gift will open up doors for
you.

Speak greatness over yourself.

You know what's worse than dying? Being alive and uninspired.

Greatness is finding something you're good at, and you keep getting better in it ... day after day, month after month, year after year.

Show me a grateful person and
I'll show you a blessed person.

Every day we have a chance to create our legacies, day-by-day it's a process of legacy building.

Let's impose our will, let's operate with integrity, and let's do our best always!

Whatever you do, make sure you do it with all of your mind, body, and soul. I believe the reason we experience so many unnecessary failures, is this... we don't pour our all into what we do. That goes for our marriages, our businesses, and our ideas. Put your all into everything you do and that'll become your legacy.

Some people want a lifestyle change, while others are living a lifestyle change.

Start living your dreams.

If you're going to the top, then selectively carry others with you.

Your temporary defeat is a part
of your long-term success.

You never accomplish true
success alone.

RELIGIOUS
QUOTES

THE TIME WE HAVE ON EARTH IS SO SMALL BUT ETERNITY IS FOREVER. REMEMBER WHAT COUNTS.

THE CLOSER YOU GET TO GOD THE MORE COMPASSION YOU WILL HAVE FOR PEOPLE AND THEIR SITUATIONS.

IF YOU SAY YOU LOVE CHRIST, THEN YOU START BY DISPLAYING HIS LOVE TOWARDS OTHERS.

MAY HOLINESS BE OUR
MARK, NOT WEALTH,
BUT TRUE HOLINESS.

LOVE TO LIVE HOLY.

MAY YAHWEH GIVE US
A HUNGER FOR HIS
WORD. SECOND BY
SECOND, MINUTE BY
MINUTE, HOUR BY
HOUR, DAY AFTER DAY,
WEEK AFTER WEEK,
MONTH AFTER MONTH,
YEAR AFTER YEAR,
AMEN.

MAY WE GLORIFY HIS
NAME.

WHEN YOU SEE YOUR BROTHER OR SISTER FALLING, PICK THEM UP WITH DAILY PRAYER.

WE WANT THE
BLESSINGS OF YAHWEH
(GOD) WITHOUT BEING
STRETCHED. ANOTHER
WORD FOR STRETCHED
IS FAITH. WE WANT
GOD'S BLESSINGS
WITHOUT OPERATING IN
FAITH.

You want to find your complete joy through GOD and His way of living. When you find joy in GOD and His principles, it balances out your life. Otherwise, if you plan to find your complete joy in people you will be sadly disappointed.

GOD WILL CREATE A VOID IN YOUR LIFE THAT ONLY HE CAN FILL.

MOST PEOPLE THINK
SEX AND MONEY ARE
THE TWO MOST
FULFILLING THINGS IN
LIFE. BOTH OF THOSE
HAVE THEIR PLACE,
RESPECTFULLY. BUT IT'S
NOTHING MORE
FULFILLING THAN THE
PEACE OF GOD.

YOU WILL NEVER MEET
A PERSON WHO HAS
STINKING THINKING
AND JOY AT THE SAME
TIME. THE TWO DON'T
MIX.

THINK ON HEAVENLY THINGS.

IF YOU DON'T HAVE IT RIGHT NOW, THEN THAT DOESN'T MEAN YOU WILL NEVER GET IT. GOD HAS A PROCESS, BE PATIENT.

DON'T GIVE SATAN AN INCH, BECAUSE IF YOU DO HE WILL TAKE A MILE.

Faith Quotes

DESIRE FAITH LIKE
A CHILD BECAUSE
THEY BELIEVE
THEY CAN DO
ANYTHING.

SOMETIMES THE
WAY IN WHICH WE
GROW UP - BE IT
OUR
ENVIRONMENT OR
EVEN OUR FAMILY
- CAN HANDICAP
OUR FAITH.

SOMETIMES YOUR
MIND WON'T
COMPREHEND
YOUR FAITH
LEVEL.

WILL POWER
MIXED WITH FAITH
IS SUPERNATURAL.

OBEDIENCE AND
FAITH RUN HAND
IN HAND, YOU
CAN'T FAKE
EITHER.

About the Author

DeAnthony Thompson is the co-founder of a charity in the Dallas/Fort Worth, Texas area called Faith Walkers Charities. He is also a radio show producer in the Dallas area and has produced the Dr. Robert Ashley Show, The James Fortune Show and currently produces The Willie Moore Jr. Show its affiliate station KHVN 970 AM.

Thompson is passionate about GOD, family and wisdom. He is a motivational speaker who believes every human has the ability to inspire, help and motivate the next generation. Thompson believes it is his duty as a young man to lead and direct those under him in the way of wisdom. He believes in the Holy Bible, and in the book of Proverbs. To book him to speak at your local church, school or establishment email or contact him at DeAnthonyThompson21@yahoo.com or at FaithWalkers15@gmail.com.

Made in the USA
Las Vegas, NV
12 July 2021

26333460R00090